The Arts: Dance, Music, Theater, and Fine Art

Earning $50,000–$100,000 with a High School Diploma or Less

Earning $50,000–$100,000
with a High School Diploma or Less

The Arts:
Dance, Music,
Theater, and Fine Art

CONNOR SYREWICZ

MASON CREST

Mason Crest
450 Parkway Drive, Suite D
Broomall, PA 19008
www.masoncrest.com

Printed in the United States of America.

First printing
9 8 7 6 5 4 3 2 1

Series ISBN: 978-1-4222-2886-9
ISBN: 978-1-4222-2888-3
ebook ISBN: 978-1-4222-8924-2

The Library of Congress has cataloged the
          hardcopy format(s) as follows:

                Library of Congress Cataloging-in-Publication Data

Syrewicz, Connor.
  The arts: dance, music, theater, and fine art / Connor Syrewicz.
      pages cm. – (Earning $50,000 - $100,000 with a high school diploma or less)
  Includes bibliographical references and index.
  ISBN 978-1-4222-2888-3 (hardcover) – ISBN 978-1-4222-2886-9 (series) – ISBN 978-1-4222-8924-2 (ebook)
  1. Arts–Vocational guidance–Juvenile literature. I. Title.
  NX163.S96 2014
  700.23–dc23
                        2013015571

Produced by Vestal Creative Services.
www.vestalcreative.com

Contents

CHAPTER 1

Careers Without College

"The starving artist" is a well-known character in American culture. She's the person who sacrifices material needs such as food or shelter in order to live a life dedicated to art. This isn't just a myth.

Dylan Thomas, for example, a Welsh poet who became very famous during his lifetime and published many successful books, intentionally chose a life of poverty. This might seem like a strange choice, but author Virginia Nicholson writes that "such people were not only choosing art, they were choosing the life of the artist. Art offered them a different way of living, one that they believed more than **compensated** for the loss of comfort and respectability."

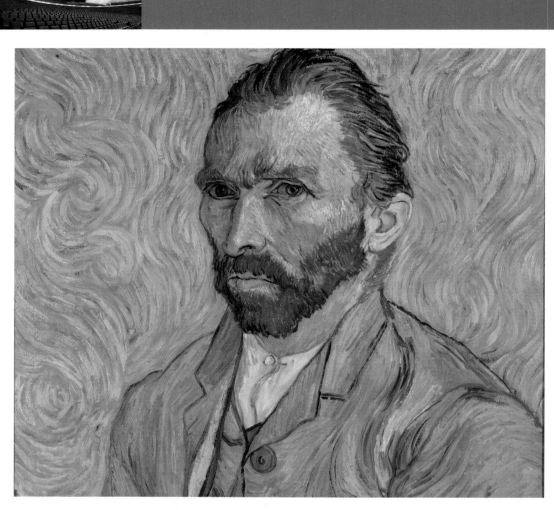

Few artists today have the artistic passion of Van Gogh, who persevered despite poverty and depression.

Choosing a life of poverty can be a very powerful artistic statement; however, the starving artist is not always "starving" by choice. Some artists have had to sacrifice material needs in order to continue to live a life dedicated to their art. Dutch painter Vincent Van Gogh, for example, whose work became very famous and successful after his death, sold only one painting during his lifetime and spent most of his life almost completely unknown and unappreciated.

Today, the "starving artist," is a character usually brought up when someone is explaining why pursuing an artistic career is a bad choice. Many people see art as a difficult field that offers little chance of material or financial success.

Few artists will become as famous and respected as either Dylan Thomas or Vincent Van Gogh. These artists are considered "visionaries"—people of great insight and skill—whose work outlived them, influencing many painters and poets after them. Most people do not have the kind of talent and luck that it takes to be remembered this way.

On the other hand, most people do not make this unlikely goal part of their definition of success! "Success" can be defined simply as "the accomplishment of an aim or purpose"—and when it comes to careers, one common way of defining success is by the amount of money that the position is paid each year.

Today, in many cases, the "starving artist" is little more than a myth or a **stereotype**. In 2011, the National Endowment for the Arts published a report indicating that, over the next seven years, job growth in the arts will exceed job growth for all other careers! Similarly, the Bureau of Labor Statistics lists over one hundred careers that are either directly or indirectly related to the arts—and most of these careers offer the possibility of making great money. Over thirty of these careers pay, on average, over $50,000 a year!

> ## Looking at the Words
>
> **Compensated** means to have made up for something unpleasant.
>
> A **stereotype** is an oversimplified idea about a particular group of people.

Photography is considered to be one of the visual arts.

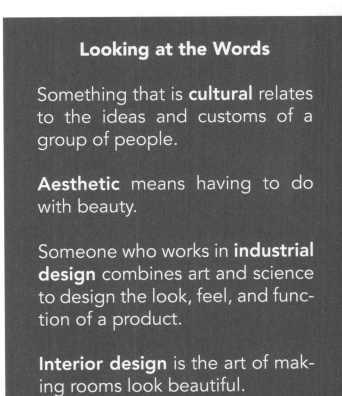

The Arts

"The arts" are a large group of **cultural** practices and products appreciated for their creative and **aesthetic** value rather than what they can be used for. Someone purchases a painting, for example, because he thinks it is either particularly unique, well crafted, or beautiful—while someone purchases a hammer because she wants to use the hammer for some purpose.

Many different kinds of artistic practices are referred to as "the arts"—painting, literature, sculpture, collage, music, dance, theater, film, architecture, **industrial design**, graphic design, fashion design, **interior design**, architecture, and photography—but while all these practices are considered "artistic," some people would take issue with calling all of them "art." "Fine art" is a term that has historically meant only five art forms—painting, sculpture, architecture, music, and poetry. But today, people are more likely to talk about the "visual" arts—any art that is viewed with the eyes, such as painting and graphic design—and the "performing" arts—any art that is performed, such as dance or music.

Looking at the Words

Something that is **cultural** relates to the ideas and customs of a group of people.

Aesthetic means having to do with beauty.

Someone who works in **industrial design** combines art and science to design the look, feel, and function of a product.

Interior design is the art of making rooms look beautiful.

Most professional ballet dancers begin when they were very young.

Many people pursue various forms of art as hobbies, but people can also build their artistic skills into careers. Pursuing these careers takes **passion**, talent, and skill. Artistic skills, like all skills, must be learned and **diligently** practiced—but one thing that most of these careers do not require is a college degree.

Learning Outside the Classroom

"Deciding whether or not to go to college was . . . tough," says Kendra Pugh, a ballet dancer who has been dancing for twenty years and has been a choreographer and dance instructor for the last ten. Choreography is the art of creating original dance routines or developing new interpretations of existing dances.

Kendra, like many **professional** ballet dancers, became interested in dancing at a very early age. Her mother, a part-time dance instructor, made a point of introducing her to many different dance styles.

"My mom," Kendra says, "is trained mostly in jazz and modern styles of dance." Jazz and modern dancing styles are known for relying heavily on **originality** and **improvisation**. They both combine different styles of dance, and they prize creative self-expression.

Kendra, on the other hand, was more interested in ballet. "My mom is loud and outspoken," Kendra says. "She needs

Looking at the Words

Intense feelings for something or someone is called **passion**.

A person who works **diligently** works hard and is determined to finish.

A **professional** gets paid to do a specific activity such as sports or dance.

Originality is the ability to think creatively.

Improvisation is the ability to do something artistic without planning it out first.

Becoming a successful ballet dancer takes years of lessons accompanied by discipline, exercise, and practice.

to be dramatic when she dances. And she has to have a certain amount of freedom over everything that she does. Ballet isn't anything like that. Most ballets tell stories, so it's not so much about expressing yourself. It's expressing someone else's story. It's about coming up with a dance that does justice to the emotion of the story." According to Kendra, ballet has a lot of rules. It is a more rigid art form because a dancer is not prized for how well she improvises but rather for how perfect her form is.

By high school, Kendra was already sure that she wanted to pursue a career in dancing, but she was unsure whether or not she wanted to go to college. "My mom wanted me to go to college," Kendra says, "but not for dancing. She would say, 'You already know how to dance, learn something else.' She was afraid that if I ever hurt myself dancing, I wouldn't be able to find a job."

Kendra's mother's concerns are not unusual. Many people see college as the best, if not the only, way to find a stable, well-paying career. This is part of the reason that in 2011, nearly seven out of every ten students who graduated high school went on to attend college.

Unfortunately a college education isn't necessarily a safe bet when it comes to finding a successful career. According to CNN the average student, in 2012, graduated college nearly $27,000 in debt, a debt that takes on average ten years to pay off. CNN also reported that half of all college graduates could either not find a job or they ended up finding a job that didn't require a college degree.

Though she didn't have a major in mind, Kendra eventually decided to enroll in a local college—but then she dropped out only a short time later. "A few months after going to college," Kendra says, "I auditioned for the leading role in *The Beauty and the Beast*, organized by one of the most **prestigious** ballet companies in San Francisco. I didn't get the part but I did get the role of first alternate." An alternate is someone who acts as a substitute for someone else in case he is unable to perform. The role of a substitute may not sound like much of an honor but Kendra had **auditioned** against many women who had much more experience than her. While she didn't get the leading role, first alternate means that she was considered good enough to be trusted with taking the leading dancer's role if she were unable to dance for whatever reason. Unfortunately, the show was planning on spending the next forty weeks touring the country, which meant that Kendra had some quick decisions to make.

Looking at the Words

A **prestigious** place or award is highly esteemed and respected.

A person who has **auditioned** has tried out for a role, often in a play, movie, or other performance.

Kendra's success took a little luck—but even more, it took time, self-discipline, effort, passion, and persistence.

"I talked it over with my mom," Kendra says, "and together we decided I should grab this opportunity. 'I can always go back to college,' I told myself." Being involved in that show turned out to be fantastic for Kendra's career. She got a lot of experience doing what she loves, danced in a number of other touring shows for the company, and even got some experience choreographing—all of which led her to the career that she has now.

Not everyone will have the chance to develop her skills this way of course. "I am lucky," Kendra says. "I had a mom who supported me. She got me involved early, and she paid for all the lessons I needed."

Kendra's story makes an important point. She spent a lot of time after school practicing her dancing and working on shows. Even when she was very young, much of her free time was spent exploring her interests and learning. She took the time needed to become passionate about something—and eventually she turned this passion into a fulfilling and well-paying career.

CHAPTER 2

What Do Artists Do?

n movies and TV shows, artists are often shown sitting around in coffee shops, having deep conversations, engaging in passionate friendships and relationships, wearing fashionable clothes, and leading exciting or insane lives. "It's not really like that!" says Antonio Berni, a musician and **multimedia** artist. "Most of the artists I know are ordinary people with extraordinary gifts." According to Antonio, lots of artists are just talented people making a living, the same

Looking at the Words

A piece of art that is **multimedia** includes a lot of different mediums, such as film, paint, photography, and sculpture.

way people with all sorts of talents make their livings in all sorts of other fields.

"When I watch movies about artists," Antonio says, "I wonder when they ever have time to work! For most artists I know, working is pretty much all we do. Unless your artwork is selling for millions of dollars, we don't have time to lead very exciting lives." According to Antonio, artists spend most of their time making art: "Art is what we do. It's how we live." But what does that mean?

"I spend a lot of time just looking at the world," Antonio says. "That's where my ideas come from. So maybe it looks like I'm just daydreaming. But when I watch an old man walking down the street . . . or a bird that's out on my windowsill . . . or maybe just the way the light looks on wet pavement . . . I'm actually working. Something I see—or hear—triggers a reaction inside me. I start putting it together with other ideas. Maybe a conversation I have with a friend—or something I read—or another musician's performance. It could be a memory from when I was a kid. Whatever it is, I've learned that I have to leave time in my life to be open to these things. I can't just produce, produce, produce. I have to suck in the world around me, and then give it time to react with whatever's inside me. It's like a chemical reaction. Something new comes out of it. When that happens, it's the most exciting thing in the world. It's why I love what I do. The hard part is what comes next—taking the idea and doing something with it. Making it real."

Antonio's art is a mixture of music, performance art, and installation art—an artistic **genre** that draws on many other artistic genres and involves setting up an "exhibition" space. While "music" is considered the art of making sound, Antonio considers music a very limited definition of all the

20   THE ARTS

artistic purposes that sound can be used for. Antonio began his career as a DJ, a particular kind of musician who uses samples of other people's music, turntables, and electronic equipment to create music that is generally played in dance clubs. He then moved out of this line of work to pursue his career as an artist, but he never stopped using sound in his pieces; he considers sound itself to be an artistic

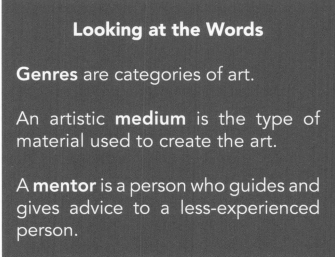

medium. His work often deals with different categories of thought, from scientific concepts to the everyday lives of people. His most recent piece is an installation accompanied by a "sound collage"—a musical technique where sounds or bits of music are strung together—focusing on a neighborhood in Baltimore where Antonio grew up.

Being a successful artist isn't just about individual self-expression. A good artist helps an entire society see reality a little more clearly; he inspires people, entertains them, and helps them face their problems. Antonio says, "My **mentor** told me once, 'If you create just for yourself, you're just looking at your own navel.' That's something that has always stuck with me. I have to express myself—but the reason I do it is for the people out there. The people who come to see and hear my stuff."

According to Antonio, artists need the ability to observe the world carefully, creativity, technical skill, and the ability to relate to a community. However, depending on your medium—the material used by an artist to create a work—how an artist spends his time can vary greatly. Art like Antonio's blurs the line between visual art and performance art, but that's still how most people think about the arts.

Visual Artists

Visual art is any art form where artists create works that are viewed, such as drawings, paintings, sculptures, or photographs.

- **Drawing** is a way of making an image using any of a wide variety of tools and techniques. Common instruments include graphite pencils, pen and ink, inked brushes, wax color pencils, crayons, charcoals, chalk, pastels, markers, stylus, or various metals like silverpoint. The main techniques used in drawing are line drawing, hatching, crosshatching, random hatching, scribbling, stippling, and blending. An artist who excels in drawing is sometimes referred to as a draftsman.
- **Painting** is the practice of applying "pigment"—a material used to change the color of something—to a surface such as paper, canvas, or a wall. Paint is often applied to a surface using a brush, however other tools such as knives, sponges, and airbrushes may also be used. Most painters are also very skilled at drawing. This is because composition—the placement or arrangement of visual elements on a surface—of a painting can take a lot of planning before a painter even begins to paint.
- **Sculpting** is the artistic process of creating a statue or a sculpture, a three-dimensional work of art. This process has traditionally meant either carving (removing material from either a large block of wood or stone, for example) or modeling (adding material such as clay to a wire or wooden frame). Historically, sculptors used stone, metal, ceramics, or wood, but since the 1800s, artists have experimented with many other materials as well.
- **Photography** is the art of creating lasting images by recording light either chemically onto light-sensitive material, such as

photographic film, or digitally using an "image sensor"—a device in a digital camera that converts an image into an electronic signal. Most photographers use a type of camera called a single-lens reflex (SLR) camera. SLRs come in two forms, mechanical and digital (DSLR). Historically, mechanical SLRs have been the artistic photographer's camera of choice. Once a photo has been taken with one of these cameras, the photo must be developed using a series of chemical baths. This process however can be time consuming, expensive, and in some cases artistically limiting. Most professional photographers today use DSLRs because photos on the digital camera can be viewed immediately after the photo has been taken and multiple photographs of a single subject can be taken quickly and cheaply. Photographers who shoot in digital formats usually touch up or modify their photos using a photo editing software.

Each one of these visual mediums requires it's own specific skill set. Antonio says, "Being a visual artist also involves a lot of skills that are not very artistic at all." For example, a visual artist will need to take care of his tools and materials. He may need to master the basics of finance and organization and do basic bookkeeping on things like income and expenses.

Successful artists also need **networking** skills, and they must be good salespeople. "A good artist," Antonio says, "is always looking for new places to show their art. You can be the best artist in the world,

Having a show at an art gallery is a great way for an artist to promote his reputation while having a chance to sell his work.

but you're never going to make any money unless you can find a way to get people to see your stuff. To make money, you have to have a certain mindset. You got to always be looking for new ways to get exposure." The better known an artist is, the more money he may be able to make.

Art in Unusual Mediums

Some artists have attempted to push the boundaries of what art is by working in unusual mediums. Art has been made using just about every material that you can think of, from tires, to old computer parts, to body fluids, to coat hangers, to food and bread, to bubblegum!

Networking skills can also lead to commissioned work. Art has been "commissioned" when individuals or organizations pay artists to produce works of art specifically for them. Commissioned art is a great way of making money as an artist, but Antonio says there are also drawbacks. "It's always a toss up when you get offered a commission," he says. "On the one hand, it's hard to turn down the money. But on the other hand, the guy offering you a commission may not have the same ideas I do about what the project should look like. Unless you have a really big name, you don't have the same creative freedom with commissioned work. You could end up compromising your own creativity, maybe even hurting the name you're trying to build for yourself. It's more like a job, less like art. You gotta do what the customer wants."

Making money off original artwork usually requires having it hung in an art gallery. An art gallery is a small business where art is hung and sold. Having your art hung in a gallery requires submitting a portfolio to the art gallery's owner and hoping she will consider your art sell-able. Some art galleries, known as vanity galleries, charge an artist a fee per day to hang their art but this practice is considered distasteful for a professional art gallery. Instead, most art galleries profit by taking 25 to 50 percent of a work's selling price.

Not every actor will end up as successful as Tom Cruise and Will Smith—but even big-name celebrities started out small, and they got where they are today because they were willing to work hard at their art.

Artists also need to know about the tax and business laws in their country. They need to organize insurance, apply for grants, pay bills and track invoices, and keep a record of galleries and competitions where they've submitted their work. This is the less glamorous side of being an artist— but is perhaps the most important part of taking up art as a career!

Performance Art

The community aspect of an artist's life also is even more important for performance artists—dancers, actors, and musicians. Performers work in front of audiences and, unless you're performing monologues or comedy, it's rare for a performance to have less than two performers in it. There are generally three types of performers: actors, dancers, and musicians.

- **Acting** is the work of an actor or actress, a person in theater, television, film, radio, or any other storytelling medium. An actor or actress portrays a character either by speaking or singing a written text known as a play (for theater), a screenplay (for film and television), or a radio play (for radio). An actor's most important tool is his or her voice. A good acting voice can lead an actor to smaller jobs doing voiceover or narration work for commercials, animated features, or audio book narration. An actor or actress's body is also an extremely important tool. In the context of film and theater, an actor is called on to portray a character using facial features and body gestures. Actors who have knowledge of other skills such as music or dance can also increase their marketability and the chances of getting jobs.
- **Dancing** is a type of art that involves rhythmic movements of the body, usually set to music or some other kind of audio arrangement.

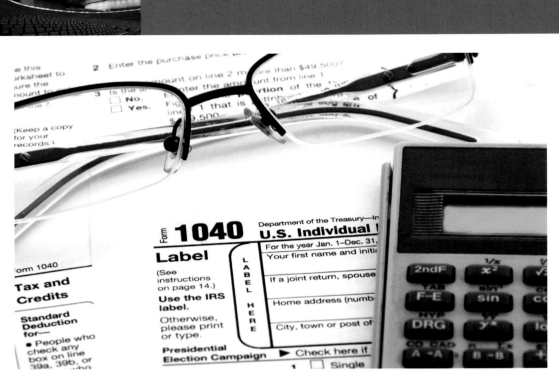

You might think that if you're an artist you won't have to worry about bookkeeping, finances and taxes—but that isn't the case! Supporting yourself as an artist, especially when you're starting out, means you have to also be a businessperson.

There are many styles of dance, and dance is often a part of other mediums such as theater or film. Some dancing, such as ballet, is used to tell a story. To become a dancer, you must be agile, flexible, and have good body tone. Training for dancers usually begins at the earliest age possible: age five to eight in ballet, usually by private teachers and in ballet schools. Students who are promising by their early teens get more advanced training. Most dancers have professional auditions by age seventeen or eighteen. By then, dancers usually focus on a specific style of dance. Dancers can spend up to eight hours a day in class and rehearsal, keeping their bodies in shape and preparing for performances.

- **Music** is an art form whose medium is sound and silence. It combines elements like pitch (the particular sound of a particular music note) and rhythm. Musicians perform every kind of music, from well-known works (often times accompanying other mediums such as theater or dance), original works (such as popular music performances), or **improvisational** music. A musician generally plays one or more instruments, whereas singers use their voices as instruments. Many professional musicians know how to play multiple instruments or styles and spend much of their time practicing or writing new music.

> ## Looking at the Words
>
> Something that is **improvisational** relates to being able to perform art or music without planning it beforehand.

Similar to visual artists, all performers must have a good handle on bookkeeping, taxes, and general finance. A career as a performer is much like running a small business.

Because many performance jobs can last as little as one day, performers and musicians are always looking for new work or new locations—known as venues—to play their music. Self-promotion, the practice to making yourself well known, can also be a very important skill, since being well-known leads both to more work and a higher salary.

The ability to network can be extremely important for finding new work. Many performers or musicians also hire agents or managers to find new auditions for them, negotiate contracts, and take care of payment issues. Managers can be expensive, but for a career like acting, hiring a manager can be one of the only ways into the business.

CHAPTER 3

How Can I Become an Artist?

"Earning enough money to support yourself as an artist doesn't just mean selling your artwork," says Sally McGill, a painter from the Hudson Valley region of New York. Sally has been painting nearly twenty-five years of her life and has been selling her paintings for over fifteen years. "You also have to sell yourself," she says. What Sally means is something very similar to the networking and community

Artistic success can be defined in different ways. It could mean fame and prestige—or it could simply mean making your living doing something you love and do well. Professional potter Laura Hanley sells the pendants she creates at street fairs and she is a pottery instructor as well. (For further information about her work go to madewithclaybylaura.com/default.php)

aspect of being an artist discussed in chapter 2; in order to sell your artwork, there is a lot of other work involved.

According to Sally, many beginning artists have other jobs in order to support themselves and their artistic careers while they are becoming better known. Whether you are a performance artist or a visual artist, she says, "You have to be willing to work other jobs. That's the only way most people can have a steady enough income to support themselves while they work on their art. Meanwhile, they also have to be working hard to promote themselves."

What makes a work of art "good" is very difficult to say. Some people appreciate the amount of skill or time that went into the creation of a work of art. Other people appreciate uniqueness, originality, or the emotional power of either the work of art itself or of the thought communicated by the work of art. "One of the best ways," Sally says, "to figure out how to make a 'good' work of art is to have understand what kind of art is selling." Sally suggests that anyone who is thinking of pursuing art as a career should research both artists whose work they enjoy and admire, as well as artists who are popular and successful today. "I know some artists who would disagree. They'd say that you're selling out if you let popular taste dictate what you create. But here's the thing—we all need to eat! And pay the rent. So I figure I can either spend my life working at something outside of art, and keep my art as my hobby—and in that case, I can paint whatever I want. Or I can figure out what sells, and support myself doing something I love. Nothing says I can't still paint whatever I want now and then. And the more people know my name and like my work, the more willing they are to accept whatever I create. But I had to play the game first before I could get to this place."

Is Working in the Arts Right for Me?

"No one," Sally says, "starts off well known—and no one starts off with all the artistic skills and marketing savvy they need to earn enough money to live on." What Sally means is that it not only takes a tremendous amount of time, creativity, and skill before an artist can begin to sell her work, but promoting herself and her work also takes a lot of time before her work will begin to sell regularly and for a high price.

"Being an artist is a lot of work," Sally says. "I have been selling my own pieces for nearly fifteen years now but it took me a few years before I made enough from my art to give up my day job." Beginning as an artist essentially means having, at first, to work two careers simultaneously. You might have to work a full-time position doing something completely different, then get home from work and spend your evenings and weekends practicing your artistic skills, sending **portfolios** to galleries or competitions, attending auditions, or spending time networking, meeting, and working with other artists.

"Lots of people take up art as a hobby," Sally says. "They can even make some good money alongside their career. But if you want to make enough money as an artist, if you want to make art your career, you

Looking at the Words

Portfolios are collections of an artist's work.

Craft is an activity involving skill in making things by hand.

have to have confidence in yourself—and you have give everything you can to your art. You need to ask yourself: Do I want to work that hard?"

A professional dancer, for example, might dedicate eight hours a day to dance and exercise—while a dancer who has another career might exercise daily and only practice a few times a week. And that's okay! You have to ask yourself: How important is my art to me? Am I good enough and committed enough to turn it into a career? Or is my art a smaller part of my life that will enrich my free time?

For those people who are interested in being an artist professionally, the Bureau of Labor Statistics lists six skills that every artist must have.

- Artistic ability. Artists create artwork and other objects that are visually appealing or thought provoking. This usually requires significant skill in one or more art forms.
- Creativity. Artists must have active imaginations to develop new and original ideas for their work.
- Customer-service skills. **Craft** and fine artists, especially those who sell their work themselves, must be good at dealing with customers and potential buyers.
- Interpersonal skills. Artists often must interact with many people, including coworkers, gallery owners, and the public.
- Manual dexterity. Most artists work with their hands and must be good at manipulating tools and materials to create their art.
- Sales and marketing skills. Craft and fine artists must promote themselves and their art to build a reputation and to sell what they have made. They often study the market for their crafts or artwork to increase their understanding of what potential customers might want.

Auditioning on *X Factor* is a dream-come-true for ambitious young performance artists, but it's an opportunity only a few will have. It takes perseverance to keep showing up for auditions that may not be as exciting—but could lead to new opportunities.

These are skills that no artist can do without. The Bureau of Labor Statistics also lists five more skills that performers and musicians should have.

- Discipline. Talent is not enough for most performers to find employment in this field. They must constantly practice and seek to improve their technique, style, and performances.
- Musical talent. Professional musicians or singers must have superior musical abilities.
- People skills. Performers need to work well with a variety of people, such as agents, directors, producers, and conductors. Good people skills are helpful in building good working relationships.

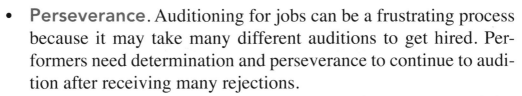

- **Perseverance**. Auditioning for jobs can be a frustrating process because it may take many different auditions to get hired. Performers need determination and perseverance to continue to audition after receiving many rejections.
- Physical stamina. Performers who perform in concerts or nightclubs and those who tour, like actors working a touring show or bands playing popular music, must be able to endure frequent travel and irregular performance schedules.

"Being willing and able to learn," Sally adds, "is one of the most helpful skills to have. You have to keep growing as an artist." Over the course of artists' careers, they should be actively seeking new ways to shape their abilities and new techniques to use. "There is nothing more frustrating," Sally says, "than being in the middle of a piece, knowing how you want it to look, and being unable to make it look that way. But that frustration is what drives me to get better, to improve my technique, to work harder."

Being able to learn is a great way to learn new techniques, but it also serves a more important function for the artist. "You can't teach creativity," Sally says. "You have to learn it for yourself." While some artists might disagree with Sally, having a strong and creative imagination is something that can't be taught by any teacher. These are traits that probably came naturally to you when you are a child—but as an adult you need to encourage your creativity and practice if you want it to grow.

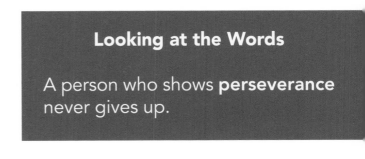

Looking at the Words

A person who shows **perseverance** never gives up.

The skills you learn in art class could open the door to an exciting and satisfying career.

Becoming an Artist or Performer

Many exciting careers involve the arts, but they require many skills before a person can be successful in this field. "Art is one of those things" Sally says, "where the best way to learn it is to do it. Begin practicing these skills as early as possible. Children are natural artists, I think—so if you like drawing as a kid, you should keep drawing. The more you use your art, the better it will become."

Beginning early also gives a performer the chance to build a résumé, which they will need to bring to auditions. Having a lot of experience to back up your talents proves you have what it takes to keep up with the grueling performance schedule of a professional show or play. Doing shows for free while in middle school and high school can be a great way to begin to build your résumé.

Artists, on the other hand, will need to begin to build a portfolio to send to galleries and competitions. This means making a lot of art, building an artistic style, and keeping good (usually photographic and digital) records of all of the art you have created and sold.

According to Sally there are many things that a young person, interested in working in the arts can do to prepare early. "Take advantage of any classes your high school offers," Sally says. "Try out for the school play. Join art clubs." Many high schools offer classes in art, dance, and theater, and most high schools host at least one play or musical a year that gives musicians, dancers, and actors a chance for much-needed experience. If you're a visual artist, a school play can be a good chance to try your skills creating set designs. Some high schools even specialize

Do You Have a Passion?

There's a lot of talk about passion these days: "Find your passion... Pursue your passion... Do what you love..."

Passion, it turns out, lives in all sorts of places. And while finding your passion is an elusive pursuit, there is only one real formula: try things. Try things and see how they fit. Try jobs and find out what you like—and just as important, find out what you don't like.

The most important thing is: Don't feel overwhelmed if you don't have a passion. Don't feel like there's something wrong with you. And then ask yourself: What is something I enjoy doing? What is something I've done already that had aspects to it I liked?

Passion can come later. Right now, just find something you enjoy. That's a starting point. Maybe it'll become that thing you can do for hours and it feels like only a few minutes have gone by. But don't put that pressure on yourself. Start small.

"Our work is to discover our work
and then with all our heart to give ourselves to it."
—Buddha

Adapted from the essay "The Truth About Finding Your Passion" by Colin Ryan. More of his work can be found at his website: http://astanduplife.com.

Modern dance performances are very different from ballet! They're often startling and meant to convey a message. Modern dance, however, requires just as much training and discipline as ballet does.

in the arts; you can learn practical artistic skills while at the same time taking classes toward graduating high school.

No matter how you get the skills that you need, the investment of time means that if you have the talent, you can be qualified for an exciting career in the arts—without necessarily going to college!

CHAPTER 4

How Much Can I Make?

ecause of the many different jobs and different ways that people in the arts sell their skills, it can be very difficult to say what the average salary of an artist is.

Sculptor Allen Freidman agrees that how much you can make as an artist very much depends on how well known you are. According to Allen, many artists begin by building a portfolio or résumé and then take on commissioned work either for free or for a small fee

Jeff Koons is one of the ten highest-paid living artists in the world. This creation of his is a puppy, 12 meters high, made completely of flowers.

in order to gain experience and build a reputation for themselves and their work.

High-Level Earnings

Allen has been an artist for almost his entire life, he says. "I couldn't imagine having any other career. I love working with my hands and I have a big imagination. Being a sculptor is the perfect job for me. I get to express myself—and I get paid great money for doing it."

Well-known artists and performers can make amazing amounts of money. Only a small percentage of artists, however, will ever perform on a Broadway stage, to a sold-out stadium, or in a Hollywood film. Visual artists have it even harder. "Works of art," Allen says, "can sell for millions of dollars, but they've usually changed hands many times before they get to those prices. And they only sell for such high prices after the artist is dead."

This isn't always the case, however. Painter and printmaker Jasper Johns, for example, holds the record for the highest price paid for an artwork by a living artist, having sold his painting *Gray Numbers* for over $40 million. ARTnews reported that the ten highest-paid living artists (who have each sold multiple artworks for over $5 million) are Lucian Freud, Jasper Johns, Jeff Koons, Brice Marden, Bruce Nauman, Robert Rauschenberg, Gerhard Richter, Richard Serra, Frank Stella, and Cy Twombly.

"They're great artists—but they're also very lucky," Allen says. "Most of us have to set our sights a little lower. You have to decide what success means to you. I'm no millionaire—but in my book, I'm a successful artist." Allen's sculptures consistently sell for a few thousand dollars, depending on the size and the amount of time that Allen put into the artwork. Between the commissioned pieces that Allen makes

Nana Miki started her career in the arts as a ballet dancer. Today, she is a choreographer who has worked her way to success.

for clients and the sales on his original work, he makes, on average, an impressive $90,000 a year!

The highest salaries for performers are even more difficult to determine because of the varying amount of jobs that the average performer works in a year. The Bureau of Labor Statistics lists the highest salaries of actors, musicians, and dancers: The top-ten percent of dancers earned over $60,000 a year. The top actors earned over $64 an hour, which, if an actor were able to work forty hours a week for a year, would equal over $133,000 a year. The highest-paid musicians and singers worked for over $60 an hour, which would equal just over $124,000 a year. Not bad!

Average Salaries

As Allen suggested, most artists won't be making millions of dollars a year—but the average artist or a performer still makes great money!

For example, according to the Bureau for Labor Statistics the average visual artist made an average of $43,000 a year. Meanwhile, how much the average performer makes has a lot to do with how much regular work he gets and in what setting he's working. For example, the average musician working in educational settings—for middle or high schools—earned only $19 an hour, which equals about $39,000 a year, whereas musicians working for performance companies—dance studios, theaters, or recording studios—earned, on average, $24.91 an hour, which equals nearly $52,000 a year. It is a similar case for individuals in dancing and acting careers. Dancers earn on average only $27,000 a year, but choreographers—the people who lead, organize, and create original dances—make on average $37,000 a year. The average actor's salary is not very far from the average choreographer, making just over $36,000 a year.

The actor Samuel Jackson is the highest-paid actor of all time.

Though these wages may not sound like a lot of money, keep in mind that many of these numbers are thousands of dollars more than the average for all careers, whether the career requires a college degree or not!

Great Art, High Prices

Depending on the artist and medium, some performances and artworks have cost hundreds of millions of dollars!

In the visual arts, Paul Cézanne's painting *The Card Players* is the most expensive artwork ever sold, selling for between $250 million and $300 million. Raphael's *Head of a Muse* is the most expensive drawing ever sold, selling for just under $48 million. Alberto Giacometti's *L'homme qui marche I* is the most expensive sculpture ever sold, selling for just over $104 million. Andreas Gursky's *Rhein II* is the most expensive photograph, selling for over $4.3 million.

In the performing arts, actor Samuel L. Jackson is the highest-grossing actor of all time, having made $7.42 billion over the span of his twenty-year film career. The Broadway musical *The Lion King* is the highest-grossing theatrical show of all time, having grossed $850 million as of 2013. Rapper Dr. Dre took home the most money as a musician in 2012, earning just over $110 million in only one year's time!

CHAPTER 5

Looking to the Future

It's hard to predict what opportunities lie ahead for artists. Unfortunately, art is often times looked at as a luxury. When a school's budget is tight, for example, art and music classes are often the first thing cut. Art is also considered an **optional** expense for businesses: During good financial years, money will be spent on artwork, while during bad years, less money is spent on artistic "indulgences."

While job growth in the arts over the next ten years is **projected** to increase faster than average for all careers, some

careers in the arts are not this lucky. Opportunities for actors and visual artists, for example, are only projected to grow by 4 and 5 percent over the next ten years, slower than average for all jobs. New technologies such as mobile and online television may eventually lead to an increase in the number of actors, but the number of

There are more opportunities today in modern dance than in ballet and other more traditional forms of dance.

visual artists given the chance at a career in the arts will be small until the world sees a significant economic turn for the better.

According to the Bureau of Labor Statistics, the number of jobs for and musicians will each increase by 10 percent, about as fast as average for all careers. The number of people expected to attend musical performances such as orchestra, opera, and rock concerts is expected to increase between 2010 and 2020, and as a result, more musicians and singers will be needed to play at these performances.

Of all careers in the arts, dancers and choreographers may have it the best. While the public seems to be losing interest in traditional dance styles, such as ballet, there is a growing interest in dance in pop culture, which is leading more people to enroll in dance school. The number of opportunities for dancers is expected to increase by only about 11 percent, about as fast as average for all jobs; however the number of opportunities for choreographers is expected to increase by 24 percent, much faster than the average for all careers.

Advancement and Skills

Other than becoming better known and more respected, advancement is a rare thing for an artist. Certain performance careers, such as dancers and actors, can advance into stage directors and choreographers. These kinds of back-stage roles in a performance require leadership skills and the ability to be a team player; however, additional training is usually required before an actor or dancer will be able to find any steady work as a stage director or choreographer.

Since most artists are self-employed, one of the only ways to advance involves acquiring new artistic skills. "Very few artists only work in

Today's successful artists work in many different mediums. The artist Beo Beyond creates light-up costumes, paintings, and photography with blacklight and fluorescent materials. (To find out more about his work, go to www.beobeyond.com.)

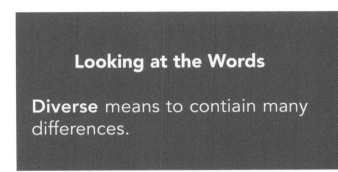

one medium these days," says actor James Mueller. In addition to his career as a semi-professional actor, James has also spent time making pop music and has taken numerous dance classes in multiple styles. "Learning music and dance added new skills to my résumé," James says. "It makes me more marketable. I can go to auditions now that I wouldn't have tried out for before."

While James is referring to the performing arts, learning new artistic skills can also be very useful for visual artists as well. Exploring new mediums can make an artist reconsider the work she does in her usual medium, and having a **diverse** portfolio can make an artist's work more appealing to gallery owners.

"Learning new skills," James says, "can be a great way to challenge yourself and make yourself more competitive. At that the same time, be careful. Trying to learn too many skills at the same time can be a mistake. If you spread yourself too thin, you'll never get really good in one area. On the one hand, you don't want people to stick you in a niche you can never get out. Personally, I don't want to be the guy who only paints sentimental houses glowing with light. But at the same time, you don't want to be all over the place so much that people can't recognize your work. You want to be known for something, a certain style. And you want to take the time to perfect your craft in one area before you move on to something else. People who jump all over the place don't usually have the discipline it takes to get really good."

Expressing Your Passion

Comedian and speaker, Colin Ryan writes:

Once you find your passion, you may feel afraid it's unlikely to come true. First, don't lose heart. Second, be careful about putting that excitement into preordained boxes—such as, "I like drawing so I must become an architect," or "I like people so I should work in retail."

There are two dangers that come from these preordained boxes. One, they can push us into something we don't really want to do. Personally, I love writing, but I discovered firsthand during two years of pretending otherwise, that being a journalist wasn't the kind of writing I wanted to be doing.

The other danger is that those boxes are often created by a culture that glamorizes fame and wealth. Here's a common example: What if you love to sing? You could tell yourself, "I better audition for *The Voice*."Instead, try thinking: "I love to sing, but I also like physical therapy. I'm going to go to school to be a trainer, and on nights and weekends I'll sing in a band or sing in my church choir." This may actually prove to be just as satisfying, as well as not quite as likely to fail. With your income needs met, you'll have a lot more time to explore your passion for singing.

(Adapted from the essay "The Truth About Finding Your Passion" by Colin Ryan. More of his work can be found at his website, http://astanduplife.com.)

Conclusion

The people interviewed in this book love what they do. They are talented and they work hard. They all had the willingness to learn more about their artform—even if learning didn't mean sitting in a classroom. It wasn't education that got them where they are today; instead, it was some combination of passion, drive, and the ability to learn that made them successful.

Perhaps just as important, they each defined success for themselves, rather than accepting someone else's definition. For these artists, success meant working hard at what they were passionate about; it meant learning all they could about themselves and their interests; it meant being able to communicate their confidence and passion to others.

For many people, college is the perfect choice and an important learning experience. Not only can it open the doors of certain careers but it is also often the first experience that many young people have at living away from home without the safety and security of their parents. It's a great learning opportunity.

Unfortunately, many students go to college with little understanding of how it can lead them to a career that they'll want to do the rest of their lives. In some cases, young people feel pressured by their peers or their parents into going to college. Many students leave college still with no idea of what they want from a career. And because of the staggering debt that many students have to acquire just to go to college, they may be in a far worse financial position than before.

Some people go to college simply because they believe they'll be able to make more money when they get out. But what good is a career if you do not enjoy doing it and are not fulfilled by it? Money is important—but if you could make just as much money or even nearly as much

Wise Words

*"To accomplish great things we must not only act,
but also dream; not only plan, but also believe."*
Anatole France

*"Happiness is not in the mere possession of money;
it lies in the joy of achievement, in the thrill of creative effort."*
Franklin D. Roosevelt

*"Commit yourself to your own success
and follow the steps required to achieve it."*
Steve Maraboli

*"Trust yourself. Follow your interests.
They will be good guides on the path of life.
Believe in your ability to follow them
with strength and purpose."*
Anne Constance

money doing something you loved, why wouldn't you do that instead? What is most important to you? What job would make you excited to get up in the morning? What career would make you feel fulfilled emotionally and intellectually, as well as give you a paycheck?

There are no right and wrong answers to these questions. Going to college may be the best option for you. Or another road might be your road to success. Either way, consider every option and be open to all possibilities. Be willing to learn and work hard, no matter where life takes you!

Find Out More

In Books

Friedman, Lisa and Mary Dowdle. *Break a Leg!: The Kid's Guide to Acting and Stagecraft*. New York: Workman, 2002.

Klein, Jacky and Suzy Klein. *What Is Contemporary Art? A Guide for Kids*. New York: Museum of Modern Art, 2012.

Raczka, Bob. *The Art of Freedom: How Artists See America*. Minneapolis: First Avenue Editions, 2008.

Watt, Fiona. *Complete Book of Art Ideas*. London: Usborne Books, 2011.

On the Internet

Artsonia Kids Art Museum
www.artsonia.com

Modern Dance
www.smithsonianeducation.org/spotlight/dance.html

National Gallery of Art, Kids
www.nga.gov/kids

Bibliography

Ellis, Blake. "Average student loan debt nears $27,000." CNNMoney, October 18, 2012. http://money.cnn.com/2012/10/18/pf/college/student-loan-debt/index.html (accessed March 18, 2013).

Kingkade, Tyler. "Mitt Romney's Debate Claim on College Grad Unemployment Was Almost Accurate." The Huffington Post. October 17, 2012. http://www.huffingtonpost.com/2012/10/17/mitt-romney-college-graduate-unemployment-jobs_n_1973765.html (accessed Mark 20, 2013).

Nicholson, Virginia. *Among the Bohemians: Experiments in Living 1900–1939*. New York: Penguin, 2003.

Thomas, Kelly Devine. "The Most Expensive Living Artists." ARTnews, May 1, 2005. http://www.artnews.com/2004/05/01/the-10-most-expensive-living-artists/ (accessed March 22, 2013).

U.S. Bureau of Labor Statistics. "Actors." http://www.bls.gov/ooh/entertainment-and-sports/actors.htm (accessed March 21, 2013).

U.S. Bureau of Labor Statistics. "Craft and Fine Artists." http://www.bls.gov/ooh/arts-and-design/craft-and-fine-artists.htm (accessed March 20, 2013).

U.S. Bureau of Labor Statistics. "Dancers and Choreographers." http://www.bls.gov/ooh/entertainment-and-sports/dancers-and-choreographers.htm (accessed March 20, 2013).

U.S. Bureau of Labor Statistics. "Independent Artists, Writers, and Performers." http://www.bls.gov/oes/current/naics4_711500.htm (accessed March 19, 2013).

U.S. Bureau of Labor Statistics. "Musicians and Singers." http://www.bls.gov/ooh/entertainment-and-sports/musicians-and-singers.htm (accessed March 20, 2013).

Index

About the Author

Connor Syrewicz is a writer and editor from Binghamton, New York. He was raised on Long Island, has a degree in English, and spends most of his time writing and facilitating other creative projects. His interests include art and philosophy, which he actively incorporates into his writing.

Picture Credits